a teachable moment book

we're running late!

teachable moments for working mothers

kass p. dotterweich

LIGUORI
PUBLICATIONS

One Liguori Drive
Liguori, MO 63057-9999
(314) 464-2500

Published by Liguori Publications
Liguori, Missouri 63057-9999

Library of Congress Cataloging-in-Publication Data

Dotterweich, Kass P.
    We're running late! : teachable moments for working moms /
by Kass P. Dotterweich. — 1st ed.
        p.   cm. — (A teachable moment book)
    ISBN 0-89243-924-6 (pbk.)
    1. Working mothers. 2. Parenting. I. Title. II. Series.
HQ759.48.D685 1996
649'.1—dc20   96-4571

Dedication

To all baby-sitters
and childcare providers.

Contents

Introduction

Late suppers, massive pools of clutter, last-minute searches for lost items, complicated schedules, childcare concerns: these are just a few of the countless challenges we working mothers face on a regular basis. Our day begins early, ends late, and disappears into yesterday—and what wasn't taken care of yesterday greets us again today as the alarm catapults us to our feet for another day.

Often, in the midst of our hectic routine, we hear that soft voice in the back of our mind tugging at our heart: "Am I shortchanging my kids? Am I being the best mother I can be? Am I missing something? Are my children missing something?" For many of us, these questions remain rhetorical because our working is necessary for survival. For others, those of us who choose to work for reasons other than financial, these questions become somewhat philosophical, but nonetheless significant.

We working mothers cannot be one-hundred-percent mother and one-hundred-percent woman of the work force. An inherent tension exists between parenting and working, a tension that, for our own individual reasons, we befriend. Some of us succeed at balancing our routines, some of us manage, and some of us—well, some of us will just never know the meaning of *balance* or *manage.*

Fortunately, the time we do spend with our children is pregnant with potential "teachable moments": those countless opportunities we can use to teach human values, practical-living values, or faith values.

What Is a Teachable Moment?

No distinct characteristics specifically identify a teachable moment. No time of day, location, or situation universally presents itself as prime for teaching. If such hallmarks for teachable moments did exist, all working mothers would be readily equipped to seize the rich opportunity when a moment proclaimed, "Here I am: a teachable moment!"

Yet, even without hallmarks, the teachable moment is recognized by the hearts of mothers seriously invested in their children's lives—for the teachable moment is *now*! Regardless of your workload, your hours, or the amount of time you have to spend with your children, the teachable moment is *here*, waiting to be mined.

Perhaps that seems overwhelming. After all, the chaotic, often tense and stressful day-in, day-out life of working and parenting is demanding enough without adding teachable moments all over the place. To think that every moment with our children is packed with opportunities to teach them something can leave us mentally and emotionally exhausted. Keeping the kids healthy and emotionally and physically safe, educating them, and giving them a faith foundation are demanding enough.

But wait! It isn't that overwhelming at all—because we *choose* the moments we seize as "teachable." Through a thoughtful awareness for our children's overall well-being—physical, emotional, and spiritual—we can select those moments when a value can be taught or reinforced with nothing more than a few simple comments or casual gestures.

Using the Teachable Moment

As you select the teachable moments in your child's life, there are a few guidelines to keep in mind.

- Don't expect results immediately or even in the near future. Teachable moments are long-term investments; it may be months—perhaps years—before you notice something in your child that indicates a teachable moment has paid off.

- The teachable moment is not the lead-in for a lecture. To overdo the moment is to teach something you have no intention of teaching.

- Keep the exchange light, using humor whenever possible.

- If your child becomes tense, argumentative, or defensive, tactfully bring closure to the exchange. The idea is to plant a seed of practical or spiritual wisdom, not to prove a point, modify behavior, criticize, or solve a problem.

- The following moments are adaptable to any child, regardless of his or her age. Use your imagination to tailor the exchange to your child's level of maturity and understanding, taking into consideration the particular circumstances of the moment.

- A few of the moments offer suggestions for what to say; take them as just that: *suggestions.* You've been talking with your child longer than anyone, so you know best how to express what you want to say. The verbatim sections are offered merely as tools to use and adapt as you see fit.

- While mining teachable moments, keep in mind that you are co-creating with God in the growth process of your child. As a working mother, always start from a positive stance: "I am doing the best I can and so is my child."

"I Don't Want to Go!"

The Moment

Sometimes you anticipate it because it has become a daily complaint; other times, it comes as a surprise: "I don't want to go!" When your child doesn't want to go to school/baby-sitter/day care, the usual challenging routine takes on one more detail that demands your attention. Seize the moment

- to show your child that you hear the emotion being expressed

- to emphasize the value of community and the important role your child plays in the lives of others

The Lessons

When your child doesn't want to go, respond with something that indicates you've heard, that you understand, and that you're sorry your child is unhappy. That's all. This is not a time to review the household budget—"Mom has to work because we need the money"—to criticize the child for failing to cooperate—"I don't have time for this"—or to threaten with unpleasant alternatives—"If you don't go, then…."

Direct your child's attention to the care and kindness of the people who will interact with him or her throughout the day. Comment on how fortunate you feel that others in the community care for your child in very special ways.

Affirm your child in the social role he or she plays in the lives of others. Point out how much other children and adults look forward to being with the very special person your child is; tell your child how others actually plan for his or her presence with lesson plans, meals, or special activities. Sensing that you have heard and understood your child, he or she is now ready to hear and understand you.

"I Can't Find My Car Keys!"

The Moment

As you buckle the seat belts and secure your child in the car, you dig for your keys—somewhere in the collection of oddities and used tissues at the bottom of your purse. The first flash of fear is quickly followed by a deep sigh of resignation: "I can't find my car keys." Before the moment becomes polluted with frantic frustration, seize it to teach your child

- his or her role in looking for a misplaced item

- that parents can make mistakes and misplace things as easily as kids

"I Can't
Find My
Car Keys!

The Lessons

Once you realize that you don't have your keys, invite your child to help you look for them. While emphasizing the task and the fun of hunting for something, divide the hunt into small bites: "You check the bedrooms; I'll check the kitchen and living room." Express your appreciation for your child's participation. Mention to your child that you know children often notice things that adults don't—so maybe he or she will be able to locate the keys with little effort. Draw your child's attention to the fact that something so small and relatively inexpensive can have great value, and thus the hunt is worth the effort.

During the search, tell your child that kids lose and misplace things all the time and parents get frustrated, sometimes angry—but that these same parents often forget that they can be just as careless. Point out to your child how good it is for parents to be reminded of the mistakes they make, mistakes they often don't notice. You might want to apologize to your child for any inconvenience he or she may experience because you misplaced your keys.

"I Lost My House Key!"

The Moment

The statement shatters the quiet time when you finally catch your breath at the end of the day, or it fragments the pace of your no-nonsense morning routine. Your child, a latchkey child, admits that he or she has lost the house key. Seize the moment

- to teach your child the difference between a *lost* and a *misplaced* item

- to model a logical method of looking for a lost item

- to affirm your child in the many ways he or she is usually responsible

"I Lost My
House Key!"

The Lessons

This is not the time to review your child's history of losing or misplacing things. Tell your child that *lost* means the key is somewhere "out there" in the broader world: at school, on the bus, on the playground—meaning it is indeed lost and there's little use in looking for it. On the other hand, *misplaced* means that the key is "somewhere" at hand, just not where it usually is.

Offer your child a model for looking for lost or misplaced items, starting with the obvious questions: "When did you last use your key? Where did you put your key when you unlocked the door the last time? Where do you usually keep your key? Did you look there? Let's look again. Where else might you have carried the key? Have you checked all the pockets in the clothes you were wearing when you last used the key?"

Throughout the process, mention to your child all those areas in which he or she is usually responsible: feeding the dog, taking out the trash, doing homework. As you accentuate the positive, your child is assured that misplacing an item does not automatically brand someone as irresponsible.

Dying
Flowers

a teachable moment

The Moment

You're starting supper, folding laundry, or taking out the trash—when something draws your attention to the brown, drooping philodendron on the window sill. When you notice that your houseplants are suffering from a significant deficiency of moisture, seize the moment to teach your child

- the essential value of water

- a respect for all living things

The Lessons

Let your child see your immediate concern for the life of the plant by talking softly to yourself: "Oh, my! I haven't watered the flowers this week. They're really thirsty—and they won't live long without water. They need water to stay healthy."

If possible, stop what you're doing, find a container, fill it with water, and approach the plant. Smile as you slowly water the plant, and let your child hear you gently address it. Apologize to the plant, and reassure it that you'll try not to neglect its needs in the future. Then, without further comment, return to what you were doing.

"I Get the Front Seat!"

The Moment

Each morning the chorus floats out the door and toward the car, a chorus of noise and bickering: "I get the front seat!" "No, I get it! You had it yesterday!" "That doesn't matter!" Something about the view from the front seat of the car is simply more entertaining to children than the view from the back. Seize the moment to teach your child

- the responsibility a front-seat passenger must assume that back-seat passengers don't need to worry about

- the importance of a calm driver

"I Get the Front Seat!"

The Lessons

Even if the scene has occurred dozens of times before, this is not the time to engage in problem solving. (You certainly will want to address the issue at another time—preferably before the next time you load the kids into the car.) Rather, point out that the front-seat passenger has a job to do, that he or she is not just along for the ride. Explain that the person in the front seat does not get to surf the radio channels or play with the sun visors. Rather, that person must remain alert, assist the driver in noting road conditions and signs, and serve as a lap for purses, diaper bags, and the other odd luggage that Mom carries.

Make a brief statement about how important it is for the driver to enter the car calmly, without headaches and hassles, so that he or she can remain alert for the safety of everyone involved. Point out that it's especially helpful when the passengers don't argue or bicker.

Too Little Sleep

The Moment

You're moving briskly through your morning routine, but your child is sluggish, slow, perhaps grouchy. Your child was up late last night, and the effects of fatigue are evident. Your child moves slowly, doesn't focus well, and displays a lack of cooperation, perhaps hostility. Seize the moment to briefly explore

- the negative effects that fatigue has on the body

- the value of rest as part of a healthy routine

The Lessons

The reason for your child's late night is not the issue here; the presence of fatigue is. Tell your child how you see fatigue affecting his or her body and the family's morning routine. Mention your child's slow movements, inability to remain attentive to a chore or a conversation, and attitude. Avoid criticism; rather, make a comparative observation: "Ordinarily, you're awake and perky. You're ready for whatever the day brings. When you haven't had enough sleep, you don't feel well and you aren't able to be your very best."

As you continue with your routine, comment about the value of following a schedule. Point out that time is an important part of life, not only during the day but through the night as well. Emphasize that time is God's gift to us, to help us make the most of each day—and night. Suggest to your child that both of you should concentrate on the importance of including enough time for rest and sleep in your routines. Together, resolve that a late night will not happen again.

Missing the School Play

The Moment

You've just checked the school calendar, and your spirits drop; the date of your child's school play/recital/open house conflicts with your work schedule. You cannot manage to be in two places at once—you haven't yet mastered bilocation! You know your child will be disappointed, and you know, at least in this particular instance, you cannot neglect your work responsibility. Seize the moment to teach your child

- the value of telling his or her story

- the difference between priorities of the heart and priorities of the "real" world

The Lessons

Without panic, anger, or exasperation—but with a delicate measure of regret—tell your child about the scheduling conflict. As you let your child see your struggle with duty versus desire, make it clear that you will be unable to attend the function. Once you have clearly conveyed that fact and your own regret at missing the event, emphasize to your child how excited you will be to hear about the event, how the retelling of the activity will be a special time of sharing between the two of you—one you eagerly anticipate. Suggest that another important family member attend—perhaps Grandma or Grandpa, who might even take pictures or videotape the event. Encourage your child to tell you everything about the event, just as he or she remembers it, because that's what's most important to you.

Explain to your child what *priority* means, and use this situation to demonstrate how priorities of the heart are not always the same as priorities of the rest of the world. Assure your child that between the two of you, at least this time, your hearts' priorities are the same.

Missing
the School
Play

Dust in the Sunlight

DUSTBUNNY

The Moment

You sit down to catch a second breath and notice the sun flirting with the layer of dust on the television/coffee table/bookcase. Or you spy those friendly "dust bunnies" under the rocker or trapped in the corner behind the door. You moan and heave a fatigue-laden sigh. Seize the moment to convey to your child

- the difference between dust and filth

- the respect you have for your own limited reserves of time and energy

- the delight that God takes in the simplest things, even in the dust

Dust in the
Sunlight

The Lessons

Through your fatigue, let your child see you smile. Don't rush to get a dust rag; don't kick the "bunnies" around with your toe; don't comment about doing some cleaning over the weekend. Without frustration, remark, "Well, it's dust; it isn't filth—we won't get sick because we've got a little dust around the house, will we?" Your child sees you respect yourself and the limits of your time when you don't get compulsive about certain details.

Emphasize the beauty of all God's creation by noting how even the sunlight transforms a little dust into something to marvel at. If you observe the dust floating in the rays of sunlight, comment on how playful the floating dust particles seem, as they dance in God's sight.

Dust in the
Sunlight

Success in the Workplace

a teachable moment

The Moment

You've earned a promotion/raise/recommendation/ special merit award. You've worked hard, and you feel good about the recognition you've received. You come home from work feeling affirmed, valued, and personally satisfied with your contributions. You're proud of yourself for a job well done. Seize the moment

- to show your child how to be appropriately proud of personal achievement

- to emphasize your child's role in your accomplishment

The Lessons

Receiving recognition for a job well done is a valuable experience for working mothers. It validates our efforts; we feel that what we do makes a positive contribution and that our efforts are noted and appreciated. We feel good about who we are in the work force. Explain to your child what you did to merit the recognition you've received; comment about the extra effort it took on your part—and how you feel the effort was worthwhile. Tell your child that you feel good about yourself and what you've done.

Credit a certain measure of your accomplishment to your child: "Because you encourage me when I'm frustrated/tired/bring work home," I have been able to reach this goal." After all, your child plays a major role in what you accomplish in the work force, and this is the moment to demonstrate how important that role is.

Labor
Day

a teachable moment

The Moment

It's the night before Labor Day, and you're anticipating tomorrow's activities; it's the morning of Labor Day, and you're relishing a break from the usual morning schedule; it's the evening of Labor Day, and you're anticipating resuming your routine the next day. Labor Day is a government holiday worth observing. Seize the moment

- to demonstrate to your child how our nation shows its appreciation for workers by setting aside this special day

- to emphasize how special it is to have extra time to be together

The Lessons

Regardless of how you spend the day, take a moment to explain to your child the significance of Labor Day. The federal government recognizes and respects all people who work hard to provide for their families' well-being, and it expresses that respect by declaring a labor-free day called Labor Day. Briefly comment how appreciative you are of this special day.

Demonstrate your appreciation for this holiday by prioritizing time with your child. Let your child see that labor is a value in your life, but that a day set aside as a break from labor is also a value to you. Show your child how you play as an adult, whether it's a game of Frisbee, a picnic, a family barbecue, or a romp on the park playground. Your child's appreciation for labor and for the fact that you work is enhanced when he or she can enjoy you and your playtime on your special holiday.

"I Hate You!"

The Moment

The cold stab to the heart that every working mother dreads, but hears at one time or another: "I hate you!" It may come in the midst of your usual routine, during a commercial break while watching television, during an argument. Wherever and whenever it hits, it hurts. Seize the moment

- to validate your child's feelings

- to emphasize the value of being honest

The Lessons

When your child shouts "I hate you!" he or she is expressing a need for reassurance. Do not try to take your child's feelings away with words like "Oh, you don't hate anyone. It isn't nice to hate." Rather, this is your opportunity to express to your child that you hear clearly that he or she does not have good feelings toward you at that moment. Reassure your child that it's okay to have those kinds of feelings, even toward people who are important to him or her. Admit that there are times when you didn't like your parents either.

Tell your child that even though your feelings are hurt, you appreciate his or her honesty. Do this with a simple and calm statement of gratitude: "Thank you for being honest about how you feel. That's very important to me." Depending on the situation, you may want to offer your child a hug or a simple non-

"I Hate You!"

threatening pat on the arm to indicate your sincer-
ity. Your child will observe that you are setting aside
your own feelings to be loving and respectful toward
his or her feelings.

"We're Running Late!"

The Moment

Your usual hectic morning routine is complicated by the added pressure of time: "We're late!" Your child may miss the bus, you may miss the train or carpool, you may be late for work. Beating the clock could become your primary focus. Seize the moment

- to teach your child respect for reality

- to model the value of slowing down to regroup

The Lessons

Few of us working mothers like to accept that time lost is seldom recovered. Once "running late" is the obvious order of the day, let your child see you face reality. Admit you're running late and pinpoint how that happened: the alarm didn't go off, you dozed a little longer after shutting off the alarm, you took time for a phone call or an extra cup of coffee, you spent time looking for a misplaced item, you had to iron an outfit. Even if the cause is beyond your control, let your child hear you identify that cause and take responsibility for the moment.

Avoid wasting more time by bemoaning you're running late. Slow down and resume the routine as smoothly as possible. Let your child see you respect the time you do have by economizing your energy and by focusing your attention on the rituals that you will not let time steal from you: the good-bye hug, the endearing comments ("Have a good day!"), the last-minute check on essential details, such as lunch money, turning off the lights , locking the door, and driving with care.

"I Have to Be a Pumpkin— Tomorrow!"

The Moment

It's frustrating; it's challenging. Your workday is over, the evening routine is well underway, and you're looking forward to resting your head on the pillow when your child announces, "I have to be a pumpkin for the Halloween party/bring in a science experiment/make a cover for my new reading book—tomorrow!" The list is endless. Seize the moment to teach your child

- the fun and challenge of creativity

- the value of individuality

The Lessons

Ignore for now your child's poor sense of timing; to some degree, we all carry around a slow stopwatch that leaves us rushing at the last minute. Besides, focusing on the "eleventh-hour" rush only frustrates the situation. Rather, demonstrate to your child how last-minute needs can cause you to inventory your household objects to find the raw material that will "work just fine": newspapers, grocery bags, empty milk cartons, old shoes, jewelry, buttons, colored thread, shoelaces, and so forth.

As you collect the needed items, point out to your child how using imagination and materials on hand can result in a distinctive product. Invite your child to be proud of that difference.

"I Have to
Be a
Pumpkin—
Tomorrow!"

"I Want Another Mommy!"

a teachable moment

The Moment

You're caught by surprise whether your child states "I want another mommy to take care of me while you're at work" or asks "Why do you have to work?" Both indicate that your child is struggling with the fact that you have a job. Seize the moment

- to share with your child your own reasons for working

- to assure your child that your working does not make you less a mother

The Lessons

Your child's statement or question is a rich opportunity for you to be specific but brief about why you work. Be honest with your child. If you work because of economic necessity, tell your child. If you work to satisfy your need for challenge and stimulation, admit this. Tailor your response to meet your child's level of comprehension, but don't sugarcoat the truth.

Avoid phrases such as "part-time" or "full-time" mother. Rather, emphasize that you do not cease to be "Mom" while you're at work, anymore than your child ceases to be your son or daughter while at school. Tell your child that he or she plays a critical role in your being the best mother you can be by respecting the fact that you work. Explain that working is simply part of the way you "mother" right now.

"I've Had a Bad Day!"

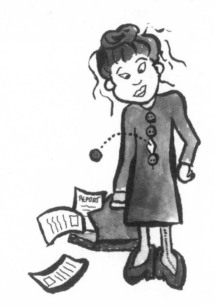

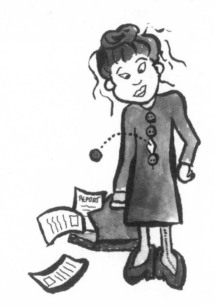

a teachable moment

The Moment

You've had a bad day. Your workload may have caused problems; dealing with your coworkers may have caused stress; your carpool arrangements may have been changed at the last minute. Whatever the source of your discouragement and frustration, your child sees you disgruntled by circumstances connected to your work. Seize the moment

- to reassure your child that he or she is not the cause of your frustration

- to model the benefits of thinking through troubling situations as preparation for problem solving

The Lessons

A flippant saying from decades ago proclaims "When Mama ain't happy, ain't nobody happy." This saucy saying contains a kernel of wisdom, especially for working mothers. Because your child is especially alert in those first moments that you're together at the end of the workday, you can teach him or her a great deal about handling personal moods. Be specific about your frustration. Pinpoint exactly what your mood is (anger, disappointment, impatience) and name the source (too much work, discourteous or insensitive coworkers, traffic congestion between home and work). Your child not only better understands your mood, but is also reassured that he or she is not the cause of your distress.

Once the specific mood and its source are clearly understood, take a deep breath and smile. Let your child see your satisfaction in that simple accomplishment. You're then ready for one of two things: with things

"I've Had a Bad Day!"

in perspective, you're ready to let go of the mood and get on with your "coming-home" routine, or you're ready to consider some problem-solving options. Your child benefits from either.

Meeting
the Boss

a teachable moment

The Moment

You and your child are walking through the mall/ out of the post office/into the grocery store when you meet your boss. Your child may or may not have previously met this person. Seize the moment

- to show your child your respect for your superior

- to demonstrate your pride in your child

The Lessons

Regardless of how you feel toward your boss, regardless of the impression you may have given your child about your working situation, this exchange requires respect and courtesy. Let your child see you display an appropriate measure of regard for your boss. Introduce your superior and your child to each other, using names first, followed by an identification: "This is (n.), my boss." "This is (n.), my nine-year-old son." Using names first presents the person as an individual separate from who he or she is or what he or she does.

If ever there is a time to touch your child, this is it. A hand on the shoulder, followed by a comment about one of your child's recent accomplishments, gives your child a sense of pride and a feeling of belonging to the identity you carry into your work environment.

"You Have Reached..."

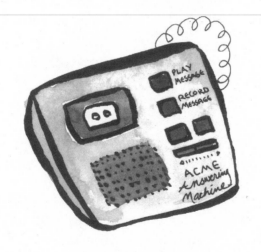

PLAY
MESSAGE

RECORD
MESSAGE

ACME
Answering
Machine

a teachable moment

The Moment

You've thumbed through the mail and now you're pushing buttons and jotting notes pertaining to the messages on your answering machine—all part of your coming-home routine. Somewhere nearby, going about his or her own coming-home routine, your child is also aware of what you are doing. Seize the moment

- to involve your child in the details of your workday

- to model for your child a system for handling the messages left for other family members

- to instill in your child an appreciation for how you must integrate your home activities with your work world

The Lessons

Invite your child to closely examine the answering machine. Briefly comment about what a major role it plays in keeping you and all members of your household informed while you're away from the house. Suggest that your child take responsibility for programming the answering message in your machine. Direct your child to be brief and precise in the message, perhaps suggesting phrases such as "You have reached….Please leave your name and number and we'll get back to you as soon as possible."

Demonstrate to your child the method you use to ensure that others in the family receive their messages in a timely manner. As you record the names, telephone numbers, and other pertinent information in the notebook or on the message pad by the answering machine, comment: "I must be careful to write the name of the person to whom this message

"You Have Reached…"

is intended." "I need to play back this last message to get the correct number." "I always add the date the message was left." Your child will see your respect for the affairs of others and will be better prepared for taking the messages when he or she is entrusted with this task.

Offer a simple comment of appreciation and gratitude for the work the answering machine performs. As you resume your routine, add a dash of humor by expressing your appreciation and gratitude directly to the machine: "Thanks for being here to get important information while we're gone during the day." Your child will glimpse the multifaceted life you lead as a working person *and* as a mom—a "working mom."

"Dinner Will Be Late"

a teachable moment

The Moment

Unpredictable schedules are predictable for working moms, but when supper will be late, impatience often reigns, for hunger is a compelling human need that must be satisfied in every daily routine. Perhaps you had to work late, you needed to run errands, or you got stuck in traffic. Whatever the reason, dinner will be late. Seize the moment to teach your child

- the value of a joint effort—family teamwork—to bring about a desired result

- an appreciation for the experience of hunger versus the experience of starvation

The Lessons

As you begin supper preparations, involve your child in your efforts. (Supper, after all, is not your single-handed responsibility.) Explain to your child that a helping hand will make meal preparations easier—though this may be a wee stretch of reality, depending on your child's capabilities—and that engaging in some productive activity will make the time seem to pass more quickly. Depending upon your child's abilities, let him or her set the table, fold napkins, or stir the soup. You might even invite your child do to some creative seating arrangements by asking, "Where do you think each of us should sit?" For some children, such ponderings can be quite entertaining, time-consuming, and pleasantly distracting.

As you prepare your meal, ask, "Just how hungry are you?" Once you hear and can rephrase your child's response clearly, briefly point out that "being hungry"—knowing a meal is merely delayed for some reason—is much better than "starving"—knowing that a meal won't ever happen. Let your child see your gratitude for the opportunity your family has to enjoy a good evening meal.

Television
Commercials

a teachable moment

The Moment

Your child is absorbed in the television set while you fold laundry/pick up the scattered newspaper/walk through the room on your way to your next task. A commercial hyping the latest toy, taste, or tool captures your child's fancy, and he or she pipes: "I want that" or "We need that." Seize the moment to teach your child

- television commercials are designed to make the viewer *think* the item is needed or wanted

- what it is really needed and wanted in life is never advertised

Television
Commercials

66

The Lessons

Be sure your child realizes that you heard what he or she has said. Repeat your child's comment as verbatim as possible, assuring the child that you're taking the comment seriously. This alone will impress your child. Briefly point out that television commercials use certain techniques to convince the viewer that a particular item is essential: slow motion, fast motion, beautiful bodies, sparkling rays of sunshine. Your child will find that curious and will watch for those techniques when the next commercial grabs his or her attention.

Without launching into a lecture, simply point out that the things most wanted and needed never appear in television commercials: love, peace, calm, respect among all people.

"I Don't Feel Good"

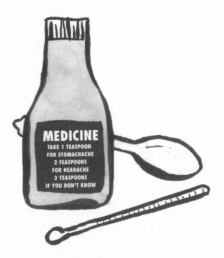

MEDICINE

TAKE 1 TEASPOON
FOR STOMACHACHE
2 TEASPOONS
FOR HEADACHE
3 TEASPOONS
IF YOU DON'T KNOW

a teachable moment

The Moment

You're going about your daily routine when your child whines, "I'm not feeling good." This may be one of the most challenging moments for working mothers because the tensions between motherhood and work world come face to face. Seize the moment to teach your child

- the value of being body-specific about illness

- the personal responsibility involved when one is ill

The Lessons

I don't feel good" describes malaise, or general bodily discomfort. Explain to your child that you need to know more about his or her "not feeling well" to be able to help. Invite your child to be specific about pain: where it is, what it feels like, how intense it is, how long he or she has suffered the discomfort. Let your child see your concern for all the details he or she offers; next, assess your child's condition, relying on your own good judgment.

At the same time, invite your child to assume some responsibility by honestly answering your questions: "Do you feel ill enough to stay home?" "Do you feel ill enough to see the doctor?" "Do you want to go on with your routine and call me if you begin to feel worse?" Tell your child that he or she must help you make decisions about what to do regarding school, the baby-sitter, and work—emphasizing all the details that must be considered. Ultimately, of course, you will make the decision that you think is best for your child. In the process of reaching that decision, your child will see you put his or her well-being ahead of any accompanying inconveniences.

"I Lost My Job"

The Moment

Unemployment affects a household in many different ways. It may be expected and thus planned for. It may come with surprise, causing panic, anger, and confusion. Loss of work affects your child as well. Seize the moment

- to share with your child the facts of the situation

- to show how a hopeful attitude can turn the end of one thing into the beginning of something even better

The Lessons

Your child will be influenced by your emotions. If you're angry, scared, and confused, your child will internalize these same emotions. Help your child keep things in perspective by offering as many details as are appropriate. Even if you were fired, it is better to be direct and honest with your child about this than it is to allow your child to draw conclusions that will impact his or her own future attitudes toward work, especially toward bosses.

Rise to the challenge of accentuating the positive. Emphasize how certain household routines will be different for a while and that the difference may actually be exciting. Assure your child that you are hopeful and excited about the prospect of change and that your lost job does not spell tragedy for your household. Your self-confidence conveys to your child that your work does not define your worth.

Grocery Shopping

The Moment

You and your child are cruising the grocery-store aisles, getting a few items on your way home or doing the week's food shopping for the family. Seize the moment to teach your child

- the importance of planning menus and meal preparation tasks

- the discipline of a food budget

The Lessons

The entire process—for many of us, the ordeal—of grocery shopping presents an opportunity for your child to see you anticipate the daily routine of meal preparation. Make occasional comments about the advantage of a certain purchase: "This is quick and nutritious." "I can put this in the crock pot before we leave in the morning." "This is something you can help me fix."

Let your child see your awareness of a budget. Comment about the weight, number of items in a package, and cost, emphasizing that the purchase of one brand rather than another—whether cereal, soup, or bathroom tissue—does make an economic difference.

Payday

a teachable moment

The Moment

It's payday! Your child knows it's payday because you go to the bank, buy groceries, do miscellaneous shopping, or spend extra time at the kitchen table paying bills. Or perhaps you're simply very direct and open about the fact: "I got paid today." Payday is important in every household, and your child senses its significance. Seize the moment to teach your child

- the satisfaction of earning money

- the responsibilities of spending money

- the role your child plays in both

The Lessons

This is not the time to critique your income. Whether or not you feel justly compensated for the work you do is not the issue. You simply want to emphasize both the privilege and the responsibility inherent in managing the financial resources that support your household. Let your child see you display some measure of personal pride and satisfaction in the contribution you make with your paycheck. A simple comment, "I work hard, and I'm glad that my hard work makes a difference to our family," reveals your pride and your gratitude.

Many parents prefer to withhold the amount of their income, and that's reasonable. After all, "how much" is less significant than the fact that your working contributes to your family's well-being. You don't need to list your accounts payable to impress upon your child the responsibility involved in spending your paycheck. Simply mention that a portion of your paycheck "has already been spent" for important conveniences and comforts: the electric bill, the phone bill, and so forth. To those expenditures, however, suggest a special ritual that designates payday as something everyone looks forward to, something that everyone contributes to (through cooperation), and something that everyone can enjoy. This ritual may be something extravagant, such as purchasing a luxury or an expensive necessity, or something simple, such as buying a candy bar at the local convenience store. When your child feels significant on payday, he or she gains a greater respect for the fact that "Mom works."

Clutter

The Moment

You've opened the closet door to put something away, but a pile of "stuff" has cascaded to the floor where it lies jumbled and mysterious. Or you've finished preparing supper, but the clutter all over the table makes setting the table impossible. Your deep sigh alerts your child to the situation. Seize the moment to emphasize

- the importance of organization

- the respect that everyone's "stuff" deserves

The Lessons

Every working mother knows about clutter and "stuff," that accumulation of personal belongings, mail, toys, and miscellaneous treasures that simply don't seem to have any place to "be," no place to "be put." Follow your sigh with a quick comment about organization and a few swift movements that bring a small measure of order to the mess. Let your child see and hear you make a statement about the efficiency that organization brings to running the household smoothly.

At the same time, respect each item of clutter and "stuff." Don't call it "junk"—unless it is, in which case, let your child see you promptly discard the item. This is not the time to pull out the adage "A place for everything, and everything in its place," for we all know that some things exist that are important, that are needed, but that simply don't have a "place." Your child needs to see you respect the mess.

Bringing Workplace Anger Home

The Moment

Your child has been listening to you complain about a coworker who is rude/incompetent/lazy; you're pinpointing these shortcomings to vent your own frustration, not to offer information to your child. Seize the moment

- to teach your child the value of sharing and expressing your emotions

- to indicate to your child that you trust his or her ability to respect confidences

The Lessons

You didn't plan to put all your frustrations out there for your child to hear; your intense ire simply seeped out. Make eye contact with your child and smile. Let your child see that you feel slightly embarrassed about venting. Explain that sharing your emotions with your child, however, is something you value: "Thanks for listening."

Reinforce both the need for confidence—"What I've said shouldn't be repeated"—and that you trust your child with confidential information—"It's good to know I can trust you." Your child will feel a rush of respect for the parent-child relationship you share, will experience firsthand the meaning of confidentiality, and will learn a valuable lesson he or she can carry into the workplace years later: frustration is part of having a job.

"Can I Have a Lemonade Stand?"

The Moment

Your child feels the stirrings of entrepreneurship: "Can I have a lemonade stand?" "Can I have a back-yard circus?" "Can I have a yard sale?" Your child is excited, energized, and determined. Seize the moment

- to educate your child about the basic details of working

- to help your child recognize and appreciate the importance of motivation

The Lessons

You don't want to dampen your child's enthusiasm, energy, and creativity. At the same time, you don't want to assume responsibility that is better shouldered by your child as he or she learns about the world of work. Start with simple, practical questions about basic details: How? Where? When? Clearly convey to your child that you expect specific answers about supplies (which means advance investment) and location and time (which respects the neighborhood—and the neighbors). Do not reproach your child for failing to have considered these details earlier.

The last—and perhaps most important—question is: Why? Your child's motivation will influence the lessons he or she will learn. If "to get money" is your child's number one goal, do not be critical. As a person in the work force, you know that needing or wanting money is a powerful motive. But you know that other motives are also valid, even if your own situation doesn't allow such considerations. For example, mention to your child the importance of enjoying one's work, of relishing the pride and satisfaction when one provides needed services or goods. Your loving interrogation allows your child to glimpse the realities of "work."

"Can I
Have a
Lemonade
Stand?"

"I Want You to Be a Room Mother"

a teachable moment

The Moment

The school year has just begun and your child brings home all the usual paperwork, including an invitation for you to be a room mother. Your child is excited about the idea and urgently asks you to accept. Seize the moment

- to show your child how his or her school values the same things you value

- to express your appreciation for those parents who accept the room-mother invitation

The Lessons

Most children, especially younger ones, enjoy having Mom participate in school-related activities, such as chaperoning, joining the PTO, and serving as room mother. A simple comment, "It's important for the school to include parents in the things that go on at school," will indicate to your child that you share the same values as the teachers and the principal at your child's school. When a child sees home values and school values reflecting each other, he or she senses the common purpose between the two.

At the same time, briefly comment about your limited time and energy, emphasizing that your "spare" time must be focused on being mother to your child. Offer a simple statement of gratitude for those who are willing and able to accept the room-parent responsibilities.

"Can I Mow the Lawn?"

GRASS ATTACKER

a teachable moment

The Moment

You're trying to squeeze in one more of those pressing chores so familiar to a mother in the work force when your child unexpectedly asks, "Can I mow the lawn?" "Can I do the laundry?" "Can I vacuum?" "Can I wash the car?" Whatever the offer, it involves something your child has never done. Seize the moment

- to celebrate a rite of passage with your child

- to reinforce your child's desire to try something new

- to emphasize the joy of an unexpected helping hand

The Lessons

Your child has never mowed the lawn/done the laundry/run the vacuum/washed the car—has never made such an offer! He or she may wish to be helpful, may be bored and wants to do something different, or may be excited by the challenge of handling the mower/washing machine/vacuum cleaner/water hose. (This often happens after the purchase of a piece of equipment.) This is a moment of passage for your child. Stop what you're doing and, with surprise, observe: "This is new. You've never done this before. You're growing up."

Depending on your child's abilities, briefly discuss the details—especially the safety precautions involved—and encourage your child to proceed. Do what is necessary to help your child get started; invite your child to ask for your help at any time.

"Can I Mow the Lawn?"

Express your appreciation for the significance of this simple offer from your child. Point out how much easier it is for you, with your limited time, to be able to rely on your child to do some of the things you have to either fit into your schedule, delay, or skip altogether.

The Argument

a teachable moment

The Moment

You and your child are locked in a heated argument. The issue may be central to the exchange, or the situation simply may be rooted in fatigue, rushed schedules, a miscommunication, or a misunderstanding. Arguments between working mom and child are potent opportunities for strengthening the relationship. Seize the moment

- to teach your child the value of a disagreement

- to build respect for the hard work involved in keeping the relationship between the two of you open and healthy

The Lessons

Arguments take energy and time. Often they become battlefields where someone wins and someone else loses, or the parent simply "pulls rank" with something like "…because I said so!" Arguments, however, can be healthy and cleansing. In the midst of your exchange, state the obvious: "We are having an argument. This is good." That alone may bring some humor to the situation. Let your child see that you do not fear or resent disagreements, that you welcome the opportunity to express your viewpoint and to hear your child's.

Express gratitude to your child for caring enough to remain engaged in the exchange: "Thank you for wanting to get this worked out." Such a comment reassures your child that the relationship you share is more important to you than the immediate issue.

End-of-Day Crisis

a teachable moment

The Moment

Your coming-home routine erupts in chaos. You face a broken furnace/disturbing message on the answering machine/a sick dog. As you rush into your crisis-management mode, seize the moment

- to teach your child that crisis and chaos do not erase your awareness of his or her presence

- to show appreciation for your usual coming-home routine at day's end

The Lessons

You're a mom, so crisis and chaos are neither new nor unfamiliar experiences. You know how to isolate the details, what steps to take. Let your child see you acknowledge the chaos and crisis that reign in this moment. Show your sense of direction and your determination to keep pandemonium at bay. State the obvious: "We've got to take care of this right now." Even if your child will not play a major role in whatever needs to be done, using "we" conveys your awareness of him or her as you manage the crisis.

Sometime during the minutes and hours that follow, heave a deep sigh of relief and express your gratitude for your usual end-of-day routine. Be specific: "It sure is nice to just unlock the door, come into the house, and find everything pretty much the way we left it." Your child will be reminded of the value of what he or she probably seldom notices: the comfort and security of routine.

End-of-Day
Crisis

The
Poke
Bug

poke bug

a teachable moment

The Moment

It's classic; your child has been bitten by the "poke bug!" No amount of encouragement, assistance, or threatening enlivens your child's movement. Getting dressed, brushing teeth, eating breakfast, mere walking—all are in a slow-motion mode. Seize the moment

- to give your child the attention he or she is silently seeking

- to affirm the value of "slowing down to smell the roses"

The Poke
Bug

The Lessons

Poky behavior is usually your child's way of saying, "I need to be the center of your attention right now." Your child knows that the morning routine is "prime time" for you, so that's usually when poky behavior occurs. Avoid "naming" or "labeling" your child's behavior. Rather, respond with what your child wants: your positive and loving attention. Mentally move ahead of your child, anticipating his or her next move, and arrange things accordingly. In a positive and caring tone of voice, mention what you're doing with each action; point out how you intend that action to be helpful: "I'm putting your shoes by the door so you can slip them on quickly and easily." "I've put your coat and gloves on the couch so you're ready to go." "I've put out your milk and cereal, so you can eat at any time." Your child has your positive attention and thus is motivated to match your stride.

The Poke
Bug

107

As you arrange things for your child, comment about the good things we notice when we slow down. Wonder at the magic of a zipper or the convenience of Velcro. Comment on the goodness of fresh, cold milk and the "music" of cereal being crunched and relished. As you redirect your child's sluggish and controlling behavior into tender, loving awareness, the atmosphere—and your child—can be energized.

Epilogue

We are legion. We are women in the work force, women active in community and church service, women in intimate relationship, women managing a household—and we are mothers. For reasons unique to each of us, we have chosen the challenge of spreading our arms wide in the world, embracing a "both/and" universe rather than an "either/or" world. We have laid to rest the old proverb "The hand that rocks the cradle rules the world" and have laid our hand to another plow: the plow of our own lives.

Many of us reconcile our multifaceted lifestyle with energy, grace, and a well-defined purpose. Some of us struggle with that inner tension that only the working mother can define. All of us, however, have the privilege of impacting our children's lives like no one else. With our daily confusions and routines, our frustrations and satisfactions, our failures and successes, we model for our children the full spectrum of life. We show our children how the world of home, family, security, and routine can coexist with the world of nine-to-five, a paycheck, a boss. We are the merging of Scripture's Mary and Martha, pausing for moments of wisdom while stirring the soup. To be sure, we may never make peace with some of our inner tensions. But we can be confident that, because we are "working mothers," our children will catch from us a gusto for life that leaves them free to push their own horizons, to define their own stars, and to bravely go where we have lighted the way—one teachable moment at a time.

About
the
Author

During the past quarter century, Kass Dotterweich, mother of six, has experienced firsthand the challenges that confront working mothers—teaching elementary school, running a weekly newspaper, and editing *Marriage and Family Magazine*. And she continues to blend parenting with working; she works full time as a managing editor at Liguori Publications, writes books and pamphlets at her St. Louis home, keeps the carpool schedule straight, and continues to mine the "teachable moments" that spring up in her busy family's lives.

Despite the logistics of getting several children to where each needs to be, maintaining a positive attitude when overwhelmed, and deciding what to do when a child is ill, Ms. Dotterweich says the struggle has been worthwhile; she basks in the values about working that her children have absorbed: their high regard for satisfying work and their pride in a job well done.

What advice will she give her daughters when they face the same challenges? "Hug your kids a lot—and talk to them a lot."